The Epistle of St. Barnabas

The Epistle of St. Barnabas

St. Barnabas

The Epistle of St. Barnabas

© Lighthouse Publishing 2024

Written by: St. Barnabas (unknown – 61 A.D.)
Edited by: Alexander Roberts, D.D. (May 12th, 1826 – March 8th, 1901)
Edited by: James Donaldson, LL.D. (April 26th, 1831 – March 1915)
Updated into Modern U.S English: A.M. Overett (b. 1960)

All rights reserved. Without limiting the rights under copyright reserved above, no part of this publication may be reproduced, stored in a retrieval system, or transmitted, in any form or by any means (electronic, mechanical, photocopying, recording or otherwise), without the prior written permission of the copyright owner of this book.

Published by
Lighthouse Publishing
SAN 257-4330
228 Freedom Parkway
Hoschton, GA 30548
United States of America

www.lighthouseebooks.com

Introductory Note to the Epistle of Barnabas

[a.d.100.] The writer of this Epistle is supposed to have been an Alexandrian Jew of the times of Trajan and Hadrian. He was a layman; but possibly he bore the name of "Barnabas," and so has been confounded with his holy and apostolic name-sire. It is more probable that the Epistle, being anonymous, was attributed to St. Barnabas, by those who supposed that apostle to be the author of the Epistle to the Hebrews, and who discovered similarities in the plan and purpose of the two works. It is with great reluctance that I yield to modern scholars, in dismissing the ingenious and temperate argument of Archbishop Wake1 for the apostolic origin of this treatise. The learned Lardner shares his convictions; and the very interesting and ingenious views of Jones never appeared to me satisfactory, weighed with preponderating arguments, on the other side.

The Maccabæan spirit of the Jews never burned more furiously than after the destruction of Jerusalem, and while it was kindling the conflagration that broke out under Barchochebas, and blazed so terribly in the insurrection against Hadrian. It is not credible that the Jewish Christians at Alexandria and elsewhere were able to emancipate themselves from their national spirit; and accordingly the old Judaizing, which St. Paul had anathematized and confuted, would assert itself again. If such was the occasion of this Epistle, as I venture to suppose, a higher character must be ascribed to it than could otherwise be claimed. This accounts, also, for the degree of favor with which it was accepted by the primitive faithful.

It is interesting as a specimen of their conflicts

with a persistent Judaism which St. Paul had defeated and anathematized, but which was ever cropping out among believers originally of the Hebrews. Their own habits of allegorizing, and their Oriental tastes, must be borne in mind, if we are readily disgusted with our author's fancies and refinements. St. Paul himself pays a practical tribute to their modes of thought, in his Epistle to the Galatians iv. 24. This is the ad hominem form of rhetoric, familiar to all speakers, which laid even the apostle open to the slander of enemies (2 Cor. xii. 16),—that he was "crafty," and caught men with guile. It is interesting to note the more Occidental spirit of Cyprian, as compared with our author, when he also contends with Judaism. Doubtless we have in the pseudo Barnabas something of that œconomy which is always capable of abuse, and which was destined too soon to overleap the bounds of its moral limitations.

It is to be observed that this writer sometimes speaks as a Gentile, a fact which some have found it difficult to account for, on the supposition that he was a Hebrew, if not a Levite as well. But so, also, St. Paul sometimes speaks as a Roman, and sometimes as a Jew; and, owing to the mixed character of the early Church, he writes to the Romans iv. 1as if they were all Israelites, and again to the same Church (Rom. xi. 13) as if they were all Gentiles. So this writer sometimes identifies himself with Jewish thought as a son of Abraham, and again speaks from the Christian position as if he were a Gentile, thus identifying himself with the catholicity of the Church.

But the subject thus opened is vast; and "the Epistle of Barnabas," so called, still awaits a critical editor, who at the same time shall be a competent expositor. Nobody can answer these requisitions, who is unable, for this purpose, to be a Christian of the days of Trajan.

But it will be observed that this version has great advantages over any of its predecessor, and is a valuable acquisition to the student. The learned translators have had before them the entire Greek text of the fourth century, disfigured it is true by corruptions, but still very precious, the rather as they have been able to compare it with the text of Hilgenfeld. Their editorial notes are sufficient for our own plan; and little has been left for me to do, according to the scheme of this publication, save to revise the "copy" for printing. I am glad to presume no further into such a labyrinth, concerning which the learned and careful Wake modestly professes, "I have endeavored to attain to the sense of my author, and to make him as plain and easy as I was able. If in anything I have chanced to mistake him, I have only this to say for myself: that he must be better acquainted with the road than I pretend to be, who will undertake to travel so long a journey in the dark and never to miss his way."

The following is the original Introductory Notice:—

Nothing certain is known as to the author of the following Epistle. The writer's name is Barnabas, but scarcely any scholars now ascribe it to the illustrious friend and companion of St. Paul. External and internal evidence here come into direct collision. The ancient writers who refer to this Epistle unanimously attribute it to Barnabas the Levite, of Cyprus, who held such an honorable place in the infant Church. Clement of Alexandria does so again and again (Strom., ii. 6, ii. 7, etc.). Origen describes it as "a Catholic Epistle" (Cont.

Cels., i. 63), and seems to rank it among the Sacred Scriptures (Comm. in Rom., i. 24). Other statements have been quoted from the fathers, to show that they held this to be an authentic production of the apostolic Barnabas; and certainly no other name is ever hinted at in Christian antiquity as that of the writer. But notwithstanding this, the internal evidence is now generally regarded as conclusive against this opinion. On perusing the Epistle, the reader will be in circumstances to judge of this matter for himself. He will be led to consider whether the spirit and tone of the writing, as so decidedly opposed to all respect for Judaism—the numerous inaccuracies which it contains with respect to Mosaic enactments and observances —the absurd and trifling interpretations of Scripture which it suggests—and the many silly vaunts of superior knowledge in which its writer indulges—can possibly comport with its ascription to the fellow—laborer of St. Paul. When it is remembered that no one ascribes the Epistle to the apostolic Barnabas till the times of Clement of Alexandria, and that it is ranked by Eusebius among the "spurious" writings, which, however much known and read in the Church, were never regarded as authoritative, little doubt can remain that the external evidence is of itself weak, and should not make us hesitate for a moment in refusing to ascribe this writing to Barnabas the Apostle.

The date, object, and intended reader of the Epistle can only be doubtfully inferred from some statements which it contains. It was clearly written after the destruction of Jerusalem, since reference is made to that event (chap. xvi.), but how long after is matter of much dispute. The general opinion is, that its date is not later than the middle of the second century, and that it cannot be placed earlier than some twenty or thirty years before. In point of style, both as respects thought and expression, a very low place must be assigned it. We know nothing certain of the region in which the author lived, or where the first readers were to be found. The intention of the writer, as he himself states (chap. i), was "to perfect the knowledge" of those to whom he wrote. Hilgenfeld, who has devoted much attention to this Epistle, holds that "it was written at the close of the first century by a Gentile Christian of the school of Alexandria, with the view of winning back, or guarding from a Judaic form of Christianity, those Christians belonging to the same class as himself."

Until the recent discovery of the Codex Sinaiticus by Tischendorf, the first four and a half chapters were known only in an ancient Latin version. The whole Greek text is now happily recovered, though it is in many places very corrupt. We have compared its readings throughout, and noted the principal variations from the text represented in our version. We have also made frequent reference to the text adopted by Hilgenfeld in his recent edition of the Epistle (Lipsiæ, T. O. Weigel, 1886).

Chapter I.—After the salutation, the writer declares that he would communicate to his brethren something of that which he had himself received.

All hail, ye sons and daughters, in the name of our Lord Jesus Christ, who loved us in peace.

Seeing that the divine fruits of righteousness abound among you, I rejoice exceedingly and above measure in your happy and honored spirits, because ye have with such effect received the engrafted spiritual gift.

Wherefore also I inwardly rejoice the more, hoping to be saved, because I truly perceive in you the Spirit poured forth from the rich Lord of love. Your greatly desired appearance has thus filled me with astonishment over you. I am therefore persuaded of this, and fully convinced in my own mind, that since I began to speak among you I understand many things, because the Lord hath accompanied me in the way of righteousness. I am also on this account bound by the strictest obligation to love you above my own soul, because great are the faith and love dwelling in you, while you hope for the life which He has promised. Considering this, therefore, that if I should take the trouble to communicate to you some portion of what I have myself received, it will prove to me a sufficient reward that I minister to such spirits, I have hastened briefly to write unto you, in order that, along with your faith, ye might have perfect knowledge. The doctrines of the Lord, then, are three: the hope of life, the beginning and the completion of it. For the Lord hath made known to us by the prophets both the things which are past and present, giving us also the first-fruits of the knowledge of things to come, which things as we see accomplished, one by one, we ought with the greater richness of faith and elevation of spirit to draw near to Him with reverence. I then, not as your teacher, but as one of yourselves, will set forth a few things by which in present circumstances ye may be rendered the more joyful.

Chapter II.—The Jewish sacrifices are now abolished.

Since, therefore, the days are evil, and Satan possesses the power of this world, we ought to give heed to ourselves, and diligently inquire into the ordinances of the Lord. Fear and patience, then, are helpers of our faith; and long-suffering and continence are things which fight on our side. While these remain pure in what respects the Lord, Wisdom, Understanding, Science, and Knowledge rejoice along with them. For He hath revealed to us by all the prophets that He needs neither sacrifices, nor burnt-offerings, nor oblations, saying thus, "What is the multitude of your sacrifices unto Me, says the Lord? I am full of burnt-offerings, and desire not the fat of lambs, and the blood of bulls and goats, not when ye come to appear before Me: for who hath required these things at your hands? Tread no more My courts, not though ye bring with you fine flour. Incense is a vain abomination unto Me, and your new moons and Sabbaths I cannot endure." He has therefore abolished these things, that the new law of our Lord Jesus Christ, which is without the yoke of necessity, might have a human oblation. And again He says to them, "Did I command your fathers, when they went out from the land of Egypt, to offer unto Me burnt-offerings and sacrifices? But this rather I commanded them, Let no one of you cherish any evil in his heart against his neighbor, and love not an oath of falsehood." We ought therefore, being possessed of understanding, to perceive the gracious intention of our Father; for He speaks to us, desirous that we, not going astray like them, should ask how we may approach Him. To us, then, He declares, "A sacrifice [pleasing] to God is a broken spirit; a smell of sweet savor to the Lord is a heart that glorified Him that made it." We ought therefore, brethren, carefully to inquire concerning our salvation, lest the wicked one, having made his entrance by deceit, should hurl us forth from our [true] life.

The Epistle of Barnabas

Chapter III.—The fasts of the Jews are not true fasts, nor acceptable to God.

He says then to them again concerning these things, "Why do ye fast to Me as on this day, says the Lord, that your voice should be heard with a cry? I have not chosen this fast, says the Lord, that a man should humble his soul. Nor, though ye bend your neck like a ring, and put upon you sackcloth and ashes, will ye call it an acceptable fast." To us He says, "Behold, this is the fast that I have chosen, says the Lord, not that a man should humble his soul, but that he should loose every band of iniquity, untie the fastenings of harsh agreements, restore to liberty them that are bruised, tear in pieces every unjust engagement, feed the hungry with thy bread, clothe the naked when thou sees him, bring the homeless into thy house, not despise the humble if thou behold him, and not [turn away] from the members of thine own family. Then shall thy dawn break forth, and thy healing shall quickly spring up, and righteousness shall go forth before thee, and the glory of God shall encompass thee; and then thou shalt call, and God shall hear thee; whilst thou art yet speaking, He shall say, Behold, I am with thee; if thou take away from thee the chain [binding others], and the stretching forth of the hands [to swear falsely], and words of murmuring, and give cheerfully thy bread to the hungry, and show compassion to the soul that has been humbled." To this end, therefore, brethren, He is long-suffering, foreseeing how the people whom He has prepared shall with guilelessness believe in His Beloved. For He revealed all these things to us beforehand, that we should not rush forward as rash acceptors of their laws.

Chapter IV.—Antichrist is at hand: let us therefore avoid Jewish errors.

It therefore behooves us, who inquire much concerning events at hand, to search diligently into those things which are able to save us. Let us then utterly flee from all the works of iniquity, lest these should take hold of us; and let us hate the error of the present time, that we may set our love on the world to come: let us not give loose reins to our soul, that it should have power to run with sinners and the wicked, lest we become like them. The final stumbling-block (or source of danger) approaches, concerning which it is written, as Enoch says, "For for this end the Lord has cut short the times and the days, that His Beloved may hasten; and He will come to the inheritance." And the prophet also speaks thus: "Ten kingdoms shall reign upon the earth, and a little king shall rise up after them, who shall subdue under one three of the kings." In like manner Daniel says concerning the same, "And I beheld the fourth beast, wicked and powerful, and more savage than all the beasts of the earth, and how from it sprang up ten horns, and out of them a little budding horn, and how it subdued under one three of the great horns." Ye ought therefore to understand. And this also I further beg of you, as being one of you, and loving you both individually and collectively more than my own soul, to take heed now to yourselves, and not to be like some, adding largely to your sins, and saying, "The covenant is both theirs and ours." But they thus finally lost it, after Moses had already received it. For the Scripture says, "And Moses was fasting in the mount forty days and forty nights, and received the covenant from the Lord, tables of stone written with the finger of the hand of the Lord;" but turning away to idols, they lost it. For the Lord speaks thus to Moses: "Moses go down quickly; for the people whom thou hast brought out of the land of Egypt have transgressed." And Moses understood [the meaning of God], and cast the two tables out of his hands; and their covenant was broken, in order that the covenant of the beloved Jesus might be sealed upon our heart, in the hope which flows from believing in Him. Now, being desirous to write many things to you, not as your teacher, but as becomes one who loves you, I have taken care not to fail to write to you from what I myself possess, with a view to your purification. We take earnest heed in these last days; for the whole [past] time of your faith will profit you nothing, unless now in this wicked time we also withstand coming sources of danger, as becomes the sons of God. That the Black One may find no means of entrance, let us flee from every vanity, let us utterly hate the works of the way of wickedness. Do not, by retiring apart, live a solitary life, as if you were already [fully] justified; but coming together in one place, make common inquiry concerning what tends to your general welfare. For the Scripture says, "Woe to them who are wise to themselves, and prudent in their own sight!" Let us be spiritually-minded: let us be a perfect temple to God. As much as in us lies, let us meditate upon the fear of God, and let us keep His commandments, that we may rejoice in His ordinances. The Lord will judge the world without respect of persons. Each will receive as he has done: if he is righteous, his righteousness will precede him; if he is wicked, the reward of wickedness is before him. Take heed, lest resting at our ease, as those who are the called [of God], we should fall asleep in our sins, and the wicked prince, acquiring power over us, should thrust us away from the kingdom of the Lord. And all the more attend to this, my brethren, when ye reflect and behold, that after so great signs and wonders were wrought in Israel, they were thus [at length] abandoned. Let us beware lest we be found [fulfilling that saying], as it is written, "Many are called, but few are chosen."

Chapter V.—The new covenant, founded on the sufferings of Christ, tends to our salvation, but to the Jews' destruction.

For to this end the Lord endured to deliver up His flesh to corruption, that we might be sanctified through the remission of sins, which is effected by His blood of sprinkling. For it is written concerning Him, partly with reference to Israel, and partly to us; and [the Scripture] says thus: "He was wounded for our transgressions, and bruised for our iniquities: with His stripes we are healed. He was brought as a sheep to the slaughter, and as a lamb which is dumb before its shearer." Therefore we ought to be deeply grateful to the Lord, because He has both made known to us things that are past, and hath given us wisdom concerning things present, and hath not left us without understanding in regard to things which are to come. Now, the Scripture says, "Not unjustly are nets spread out for birds." This means that the man perishes justly, who, having a knowledge of the way of righteousness, rushes off into the way of darkness. And further, my brethren: if the Lord endured to suffer for our soul, He being Lord of all the world, to whom God said at the foundation of the world, "Let us make man after our image, and after our likeness," understand how it was that He endured to suffer at the hand of men. The prophets, having obtained grace from Him, prophesied concerning Him. And He (since it behooved Him to appear in flesh), that He might abolish death, and reveal the resurrection from the dead, endured [what and as He did], in order that He might fulfil the promise made unto the fathers, and by preparing a new people for Himself, might show, while He dwelt on earth, that He, when He has raised mankind, will also judge them. Moreover, teaching Israel, and doing so great miracles and signs, He preached [the truth] to him, and greatly loved him. But when He chose His own apostles who were to preach His Gospel, [He did so from among those] who were sinners above all sin, that He might show He came "not to call the righteous, but sinners to repentance." Then He manifested Himself to be the Son of God. For if He had not come in the flesh, how could men have been saved by beholding Him? Since looking upon the sun which is to cease to exist, and is the work of His hands, their eyes are not able to bear his rays. The Son of God therefore came in the flesh with this view, that He might bring to a head the sum of their sins who had persecuted His prophets to the death. For this purpose, then, He endured. For God says, "The stroke of his flesh is from them;" and "when I shall smite the Shepherd, then the sheep of the flock shall be scattered." He himself willed thus to suffer, for it was necessary that He should suffer on the tree. For says he who prophesies regarding Him, "Spare my soul from the sword, fasten my flesh with nails; for the assemblies of the wicked have risen up against me." And again he says, "Behold, I have given my back to scourges, and my cheeks to strokes, and I have set my countenance as a firm rock."

Chapter VI.—The sufferings of Christ, and the new covenant, were announced by the prophets.

When, therefore, He has fulfilled the commandment, what says He? "Who is he that will contend with Me? Let him oppose Me: or who is he that will enter into judgment with Me? Let him draw near to the servant of the Lord." "Woe unto you, for ye shall all wax old, like a garment, and the moth shall eat you up." And again the prophet says, "Since as a mighty stone He is laid for crushing, behold I cast down for the foundations of Zion a stone, precious, elect, a cornerstone, honorable." Next, what says He? "And he who shall trust in it shall live forever." Is our hope, then, upon a stone? Far from it. But [the language is used] inasmuch as He laid his flesh [as a foundation] with power; for He says, "And He placed me as a firm rock." And the prophet says again, "The stone which the builders rejected, the same has become the head of the corner." And again he says, "This is the great and wonderful day which the Lord hath made." I write the more simply unto you, that ye may understand. I am the off-scouring of your love. What, then, again says the prophet? "The assembly of the wicked surrounded me; they encompassed me as bees do a honeycomb," and "upon my garment they cast lots." Since, therefore, He was about to be manifested and to suffer in the flesh, His suffering was foreshown. For the prophet speaks against Israel, "Woe to their soul, because they have counselled an evil counsel against themselves, saying, Let us bind the just one, because he is displeasing to us." And Moses also says to them, "Behold these things, says the Lord God: Enter into the good land which the Lord swore [to give] to Abraham, and Isaac, and

Jacob, and inherit ye it, a land flowing with milk and honey." What, then, says Knowledge? Learn: "Trust," she says, "in Him who is to be manifested to you in the flesh—that is, Jesus." For man is earth in a suffering state, for the formation of Adam was from the face of the earth. What, then, meant this: "into the good land, a land flowing with milk and honey?" Blessed be our Lord, who has placed in us wisdom and understanding of secret things. For the prophet says, "Who shall understand the parable of the Lord, except him who is wise and prudent, and who loves his Lord?" Since, therefore, having renewed us by the remission of our sins, He hath made us after another pattern, [it is His purpose] that we should possess the soul of children, inasmuch as He has created us anew by His Spirit. For the Scripture says concerning us, while He speaks to the Son, "Let Us make man after Our image, and after Our likeness; and let them have dominion over the beasts of the earth, and the fowls of heaven, and the fishes of the sea." And the Lord said, on beholding the fair creature man, "Increase, and multiply, and replenish the earth." These things [were spoken] to the Son. Again, I will show thee how, in respect to us, He has accomplished a second fashioning in these last days. The Lord says, "Behold, I will make the last like the first." In reference to this, then, the prophet proclaimed, "Enter you into the land flowing with milk and honey, and have dominion over it." Behold, therefore, we have been refashioned, as again He says in another prophet, "Behold, says the Lord, I will take away from these, that is, from those whom the Spirit of the Lord foresaw, their stony hearts, and I will put hearts of flesh within them," because He was to be manifested in flesh, and to sojourn among us. For, my brethren, the habitation of our heart is a holy temple to the Lord. For again says the Lord, "And wherewith shall I appear before the Lord my God, and be glorified?" He says, "I will confess to thee in the Church in the midst of my brethren; and I will praise thee in the midst of the assembly of the saints." We, then, are they whom He has led into the good land. What, then, mean milk and honey? This, that as the infant is kept alive first by honey, and then by milk, so also we, being quickened and kept alive by the faith of the promise and by the word, shall live ruling over the earth. But He said above, "Let them increase, and rule over the fishes." Who then is able to govern the beasts, or the fishes, or the fowls of heaven? For we ought to perceive that to govern implies authority, so that one should command and rule. If, therefore, this does not exist at present, yet still He has promised it to us. When? When we ourselves also have been made perfect [so as] to become heirs of the covenant of the Lord.

Chapter VII.—Fasting, and the goat sent away, were types of Christ.

Understand, then, ye children of gladness, that the good Lord has foreshown all things to us, that we might know to whom we ought for everything to render thanksgiving and praise. If therefore the Son of God, who is Lord [of all things], and who will judge the living and the dead, suffered, that His stroke might give us life, let us believe that the Son of God could not have suffered except for our sakes. Moreover, when fixed to the cross, He had given Him to drink vinegar and gall. Hearken how the priests of the people gave previous indications of this. His commandment having been written, the Lord enjoined, that whosoever did not keep the fast should be put to death, because He also Himself was to offer in sacrifice for our sins the vessel of the Spirit, in order that the type established in Isaac when he was offered upon the altar might be fully accomplished. What, then, says He in the prophet? "And let them eat of the goat which is offered, with fasting, for all their sins." Attend carefully: "And let all the priests alone eat the inwards, unwashed with vinegar." Wherefore? Because to me, who am to offer my flesh for the sins of my new people, ye are to give gall with vinegar to drink: eat you alone, while the people fast and mourn in sackcloth and ashes. [These things were done] that He might show that it was necessary for Him to suffer for them. How, then, ran the commandment? Give your attention. Take two goats of goodly aspect, and similar to each other, and offer them. And let the priest take one as a burnt-offering for sins. And what should they do with the other? "Accursed," says He, "is the one." Mark how the type of Jesus now comes out. "And all of you spit upon it, and pierce it, and encircle its head with scarlet wool, and thus let it be driven into the wilderness." And when all this has been done, he who bears the goat brings it into the desert, and takes the wool off from it, and places that upon a shrub which is called Rachia, of which also we are accustomed to eat the fruits when we find them in the field. Of this kind of shrub alone the fruits are sweet. Why then, again, is this? Give good heed. [You see] "One upon the altar, and the other accursed;" and why [do you behold] the one that is accursed crowned? Because they shall see Him then in that day having a scarlet robe about his body down to his feet; and they shall say, Is not this He whom we once despised, and pierced, and mocked, and crucified?

Truly this is He who then declared Himself to be the Son of God. For how like is He to Him! With a view to this, [He required] the goats to be of goodly aspect, and similar, that, when they see Him then coming, they may be amazed by the likeness of the goat. Behold, then, the type of Jesus who was to suffer. But why is it that they place the wool in the midst of thorns? It is a type of Jesus set before the view of the Church. [They place the wool among thorns], that anyone who wishes to bear it away may find it necessary to suffer much, because the thorn is formidable, and thus obtain it only as the result of suffering. Thus also, says He, "Those who wish to behold Me, and lay hold of My kingdom, must through tribulation and suffering obtain Me."

Chapter VIII.—The red heifer a type of Christ.

Now what do you suppose this to be a type of, that a command was given to Israel, that men of the greatest wickedness should offer a heifer, and slay and burn it, and, that then boys should take the ashes, and put these into vessels, and bind round a stick purple wool along with hyssop, and that thus the boys should sprinkle the people, one by one, in order that they might be purified from their sins? Consider how He speaks to you with simplicity. The calf is Jesus: the sinful men offering it are those who led Him to the slaughter. But now the men are no longer guilty, are no longer regarded as sinners. And the boys that sprinkle are those that have proclaimed to us the remission of sins and purification of heart. To these He gave authority to preach the Gospel, being twelve in number, corresponding to the twelve tribes of Israel. But why are there three boys that sprinkle? To correspond to

Abraham, and Isaac, and Jacob, because these were great with God. And why was the wool [placed] upon the wood? Because by wood Jesus holds His kingdom, so that [through the cross] those believing on Him shall live forever. But why was hyssop joined with the wool? Because in His kingdom the days will be evil and polluted in which we shall be saved, [and] because he who suffers in body is cured through the cleansing efficacy of hyssop. And on this account the things which stand thus are clear to us, but obscure to them because they did not hear the voice of the Lord.

Chapter IX.—The spiritual meaning of circumcision.

He speaks moreover concerning our ears, how He hath circumcised both them and our heart. The Lord says in the prophet, "In the hearing of the ear they obeyed me." And again He says, "By hearing, those shall hear who are afar off; they shall know what I have done." And, "Be ye circumcised in your hearts, says the Lord." And again He says, "Hear, O Israel, for these things says the Lord thy God." And once more the Spirit of the Lord proclaims, "Who is he that wishes to live forever? By hearing let him hear the voice of my servant." And again He says, "Hear, O heaven, and give ear, O earth, for God hath spoken." These are in proof. And again He says, "Hear the word of the Lord, ye rulers of this people." And again He says, "Hear, ye children, the voice of one crying in the wilderness." Therefore He hath circumcised our ears, that we might hear His word and believe, for the circumcision in which they trusted is abolished. For He declared that circumcision was not of the flesh, but they transgressed because an evil angel deluded them. He says to them, "These things says the Lord your God"—(here I find a new commandment)—"Sow not among thorns, but circumcise yourselves to the Lord." And why speaks He thus: "Circumcise the stubbornness of your heart, and harden not your neck?" And again: "Behold, says the Lord, all the nations are uncircumcised in the flesh, but this people are uncircumcised in heart." But thou wilt say, "Yea, verily the people are circumcised for a seal." But so also is every Syrian and Arab, and all the priests of idols: are these then also within the bond of His covenant? Yea, the Egyptians also practice circumcision. Learn then, my children, concerning all things richly, that Abraham, the first who enjoined circumcision, looking forward in spirit to Jesus, practiced that rite, having received the mysteries of the three letters. For [the Scripture] says, "And Abraham circumcised ten, and eight, and three hundred men of his household." What, then, was the knowledge given to him in this? Learn the eighteen first, and then the three hundred. The ten and the eight are thus denoted—Ten by I, and Eight by H. You have [the initials of the, name of] Jesus. And because the cross was to express the grace [of our redemption] by the letter T, he says also, "Three Hundred." He signifies, therefore, Jesus by two letters, and the cross by one. He knows this, who has put within us the engrafted gift of His doctrine. No one has been admitted by me to a more excellent piece of knowledge than this, but I know that ye are worthy.

Chapter X.—Spiritual significance of the precepts of Moses respecting different kinds of food.

Now, wherefore did Moses say, "Thou shalt not

eat the swine, nor the eagle, nor the hawk, nor the raven, nor any fish which is not possessed of scales?" He embraced three doctrines in his mind [in doing so]. Moreover, the Lord says to them in Deuteronomy, "And I will establish my ordinances among this people." Is there then not a command of God they should not eat [these things]? There is, but Moses spoke with a spiritual reference. For this reason he named the swine, as much as to say, "Thou shalt not join thyself to men who resemble swine." For when they live in pleasure, they forget their Lord; but when they come to want, they acknowledge the Lord. And [in like manner] the swine, when it has eaten, does not recognize its master; but when hungry it cries out, and on receiving food is quiet again. "Neither shalt thou eat," says he "the eagle, nor the hawk, nor the kite, nor the raven." "Thou shalt not join thyself," he means, "to such men as know not how to procure food for themselves by labor and sweat, but seize on that of others in their iniquity, and although wearing an aspect of simplicity, are on the watch to plunder others." So these birds, while they sit idle, inquire how they may devour the flesh of others, proving themselves pests [to all] by their wickedness. "And thou shalt not eat," he says, "the lamprey, or the polypus, or the cuttlefish." He means, "Thou shalt not join thyself or be like to such men as are ungodly to the end, and are condemned to death." In like manner as those fishes, above accursed, float in the deep, not swimming [on the surface] like the rest, but make their abode in the mud which lies at the bottom. Moreover, "Thou shall not," he says, "eat the hare." Wherefore? "Thou shall not be a corrupter of boys, nor like unto such." Because the hare multiplies, year by year, the places of its conception; for as many years as it lives so many it has. Moreover, "Thou shall not eat the hyena." He means, "Thou shall not be an adulterer, nor a corrupter, nor be like to them that are such." Wherefore? Because that animal annually changes its sex, and is at one time male, and at another female. Moreover, he has rightly detested the weasel. For he means, "Thou shalt not be like to those whom we hear of as committing wickedness with the mouth, on account of their uncleanness; nor shall thou be joined to those impure women who commit iniquity with the mouth. For this animal conceives by the mouth." Moses then issued three doctrines concerning meats with a spiritual significance; but they received them according to fleshly desire, as if he had merely spoken of [literal] meats. David, however, comprehends the knowledge of the three doctrines, and speaks in like manner: "Blessed is the man who hath not walked in the counsel of the ungodly," even as the fishes [referred to] go in darkness to the depths [of the sea]; "and hath not stood in the way of sinners," even as those who profess to fear the Lord, but go astray like swine; "and hath not sat in the seat of scorners," even as those birds that lie in wait for prey. Take a full and firm grasp of this spiritual knowledge. But Moses says still further, "Ye shall eat every animal that is cloven-footed and ruminant." What does he mean? [The ruminant animal denotes him] who, on receiving food, recognizes Him that nourishes him, and being satisfied by Him, is visibly made glad. Well spoke [Moses], having respect to the commandment. What, then, does he mean? That we ought to join ourselves to those that fear the Lord, those who meditate in their heart on the commandment which they have received, those who both utter the judgments of the Lord and observe them, those who know that meditation is a work of gladness, and who ruminate upon the word of the Lord. But what means the cloven-footed? That the righteous man also walks in this world, yet looks forward to the holy state [to come]. Behold how well Moses legislated. But how was it possible for them to understand or comprehend these things? We then, rightly understanding his commandments, explain them as the Lord intended. For this purpose He circumcised our ears and our hearts, that we might understand these things.

Chapter XI.—Baptism and the cross prefigured in the Old Testament.

Let us further inquire whether the Lord took any care to foreshadow the water [of baptism] and the cross. Concerning the water, indeed, it is written, in reference to the Israelites, that they should not receive that baptism which leads to the remission of sins, but should procure another for themselves. The prophet therefore declares, "Be astonished, O heaven, and let the earth tremble at this, because this people hath committed two great evils: they have forsaken Me, a living fountain, and have hewn out for themselves broken cisterns. Is my holy hill Zion a desolate rock? For ye shall be as the fledglings of a bird, which fly away when the nest is removed." And again says the prophet, "I will go before thee and make level the mountains, and will break the brazen gates, and bruise in pieces the iron bars; and I will give thee the secret, hidden, invisible treasures, that they may know that I am the Lord God." And "He shall dwell in a lofty cave of the strong rock." Furthermore, what says He in reference to the Son? "His water is sure; ye shall see the King in His glory, and your soul shall meditate on the fear of the

Lord." And again He says in another prophet, "The man who doeth these things shall be like a tree planted by the courses of waters, which shall yield its fruit in due season; and his leaf shall not fade, and all that he doeth shall prosper. Not so are the ungodly, not so, but even as chaff, which the wind sweeps away from the face of the earth. Therefore the ungodly shall not stand in judgment, nor sinners in the counsel of the just; for the Lord knows the way of the righteous, but the way of the ungodly shall perish." Mark how He has described at once both the water and the cross. For these words imply, Blessed are they who, placing their trust in the cross, have gone down into the water; for, says He, they shall receive their reward in due time: then He declares, I will recompense them. But now He says, "Their leaves shall not fade." This meant, that every word which proceeded out of your mouth in faith and love shall tend to bring conversion and hope to many. Again, another prophet says, "And the land of Jacob shall be extolled above every land." This meant the vessel of His Spirit, which He shall glorify. Further, what says He? "And there was a river flowing on the right, and from it arose beautiful trees; and whosoever shall eat of them shall live forever." This meant, that we indeed descend into the water full of sins and defilement, but come up, bearing fruit in our heart, having the fear [of God] and trust in Jesus in our spirit. "And whosoever shall eat of these shall live forever," This meant: Whosoever, He declares, shall hear thee speaking, and believe, shall live forever.

Chapter XII.—The cross of Christ frequently announced in the Old Testament.

In like manner He points to the cross of Christ in another prophet, who says, "And when shall these things be accomplished? And the Lord says, When a tree shall be bent down, and again arise, and when blood shall flow out of wood." Here again you have an intimation concerning the cross, and Him who should be crucified. Yet again He speaks of this in Moses, when Israel was attacked by strangers. And that He might remind them, when assailed, that it was on account of their sins they were delivered to death, the Spirit speaks to the heart of Moses, that he should make a figure of the cross, and of Him about to suffer thereon; for unless they put their trust in Him, they shall be overcome forever. Moses therefore placed one weapon above another in the midst of the hill, and standing upon it, so as to be higher than all the people, he stretched forth his hands, and thus again Israel acquired the mastery. But when again he let down his hands, they were again destroyed. For what reason? That they might know that they could not be saved unless they put their trust in Him. And in another prophet He declares, "All day long I have stretched forth My hands to an unbelieving people, and one that gainsays My righteous way." And again Moses makes a type of Jesus, [signifying] that it was necessary for Him to suffer, [and also] that He would be the author of life [to others], whom they believed to have destroyed on the cross when Israel was failing. For since transgression was committed by Eve through means of the serpent, [the Lord] brought it to pass that every [kind of] serpents bit them, and they died, that He might convince them, that on account of their transgression they were given over to the straits of death. Moreover Moses, when he commanded, "Ye shall not have any graven or molten [image] for your God," did so that he might reveal a type of Jesus. Moses then makes a brazen serpent, and places it upon a beam, and by proclamation assembles the people. When, therefore, they were come together, they besought Moses that he would offer sacrifice in their behalf, and pray for their recovery. And Moses spoke unto them, saying, "When any one of you is bitten, let him come to the serpent placed on the pole; and let him hope and believe, that even though dead, it is able to give him life, and immediately he shall be restored." And they did so. Thou hast in this also [an indication of] the glory of Jesus; for in Him and to Him are all things. What, again, says Moses to Jesus (Joshua) the son of Nave, when he gave him this name, as being a prophet, with this view only, that all the people might hear that the Father would reveal all things concerning His Son Jesus to the son of Nave? This name then being given him when he sent him to spy out the land, he said, "Take a book into thy hands, and write what the Lord declares, that the Son of God will in the last days cut off from the roots all the house of Amalek." Behold again: Jesus who was manifested, both by type and in the flesh, is not the Son of man, but the Son of God. Since, therefore, they were to say that Christ was the son of David, fearing and understanding the error of the wicked, he says, "The Lord said unto my Lord, Sit at My right hand, until I make Thine enemies Thy footstool." And again, thus says Isaiah, "The Lord said to Christ, my Lord, whose right hand I have holden, that the nations should yield obedience before Him; and I will break in pieces the strength of kings." Behold how David called

Him Lord and the Son of God.

Chapter XIII.—Christians, and not Jews, the heirs of the covenant.

But let us see if this people is the heir, or the former, and if the covenant belongs to us or to them. Hear you now what the Scripture says concerning the people. Isaac prayed for Rebecca his wife, because she was barren; and she conceived. Furthermore also, Rebecca went forth to inquire of the Lord; and the Lord said to her, "Two nations are in thy womb, and two peoples in thy belly; and the one people shall surpass the other, and the elder shall serve the younger." You ought to understand who was Isaac, who Rebecca, and concerning what persons He declared that this people should be greater than that. And in another prophecy Jacob speaks more clearly to his son Joseph, saying, "Behold, the Lord hath not deprived me of thy presence; bring thy sons to me, that I may bless them." And he brought Manasseh and Ephraim, desiring that Manasseh should be blessed, because he was the elder. With this view Joseph led him to the right hand of his father Jacob. But Jacob saw in spirit the type of the people to arise afterwards. And what says [the Scripture]? And Jacob changed the direction of his hands, and laid his right hand upon the head of Ephraim, the second and younger, and blessed him. And Joseph said to Jacob, "Transfer thy right hand to the head of Manasseh, for he is my first-born son." And Jacob said, "I know it, my son, I know it; but the elder shall serve the younger: yet he also shall be blessed." Ye see on whom he laid [his hands], that this people should be first, and heir of the covenant. If then, still further, the same thing was intimated through Abraham, we reach the perfection of our knowledge. What, then, says He to Abraham? "Because thou hast believed, it is imputed to thee for righteousness: behold, I have made thee the father of those nations who believe in the Lord while in [a state of] uncircumcision."

Chapter XIV.—The Lord hath given us the testament which Moses received and broke.

Yes [it is even so]; but let us inquire if the Lord has really given that testament which He swore to the fathers that He would give to the people. He did give it; but they were not worthy to receive it, on account of their sins. For the prophet declares, "And Moses was fasting forty days and forty nights on Mount Sinai, that he might receive the testament of the Lord for the people." And he received from the Lord two tables, written in the spirit by the finger of the hand of the Lord. And Moses having received them, carried them down to give to the people. And the Lord said to Moses, "Moses, Moses, go down quickly; for thy people hath sinned, whom thou didst bring out of the land of Egypt." And Moses understood that they had again made molten images; and he threw the tables out of his hands, and the tables of the testament of the Lord were broken. Moses then received it, but they proved themselves unworthy. Learn now how we have received it. Moses, as a servant, received it; but the Lord himself, having suffered in our behalf, hath given it to us, that we should be the people of inheritance. But He was manifested, in order that they might be perfected in their iniquities, and that we, being constituted heirs through Him, might receive the testament of the Lord Jesus, who was prepared for this end, that by His personal manifestation, redeeming our hearts (which were already wasted by death, and given over to the iniquity of error) from darkness, He might by His word enter into a covenant with us. For it is written how the Father, about to redeem us from darkness, commanded Him to prepare a holy people for Himself. The prophet therefore declares, "I, the Lord Thy God, have called Thee in righteousness, and will hold Thy hand, and will strengthen Thee; and I have given Thee for a covenant to the people, for a light to the nations, to open the eyes of the blind, and to bring forth from fetters them that are bound, and those that sit in darkness out of the prison-house." Ye perceive, then, whence we have been redeemed. And again, the prophet says, "Behold, I have appointed Thee as a light to the nations, that Thou might be for salvation even to the ends of the earth, says the Lord God that redeemed thee." And again, the prophet says, "The Spirit of the Lord is upon me; because He hath anointed me to preach the Gospel to the humble: He hath sent me to heal the broken-hearted, to proclaim deliverance to the captives, and recovery of sight to the blind; to announce the acceptable year of the Lord, and the day of recompense; to comfort all that mourn."

Chapter XV.—The false and the true Sabbath.

Further, also, it is written concerning the Sabbath in the Decalogue which [the Lord] spoke, face to face, to Moses on Mount Sinai, "And sanctify ye the Sabbath of the Lord with clean hands and a pure heart." And He says in another place, "If my sons keep the Sabbath, then will I cause my mercy to rest upon them." The Sabbath is mentioned at the beginning of the creation [thus]: "And God made in six days the works of His hands, and made an end on the seventh day, and rested on it, and sanctified it." Attend, my children, to the meaning of this expression, "He finished in six days." This implied that the Lord will finish all things in six thousand years, for a day is with Him a thousand years. And He Himself testified, saying, "Behold, to-day will be as a thousand years." Therefore, my children, in six days, that is, in six thousand years, all things will be finished. "And He rested on the seventh day." This meant: when His Son, coming [again], shall destroy the time of the wicked man, and judge the ungodly, and change the-sun, and the moon, and the stars, then shall He truly rest on the seventh day. Moreover, He says, "Thou shalt sanctify it with pure hands and a pure heart." If, therefore, anyone can now sanctify the day which God hath sanctified, except he is pure in heart in all things, we are deceived. Behold, therefore: certainly then one properly resting sanctifies it, when we ourselves, having received the promise, wickedness no longer existing, and all things having been made new by the Lord, shall be able to work righteousness. Then we shall be able to sanctify it, having been first sanctified ourselves. Further, He says to them, "Your new moons and your Sabbath I cannot endure." Ye perceive how He speaks: Your present Sabbaths are not acceptable to Me, but that is which I have made, [namely this,] when, giving rest to all things, I shall make a beginning of the eighth day, that is, a beginning of another world. Wherefore, also, we keep the eighth day with joyfulness, the day also on which Jesus rose again from the dead. And when He had manifested Himself, He ascended into the heavens.

Chapter XVI.—The spiritual temple of God.

Moreover, I will also tell you concerning the temple, how the wretched [Jews], wandering in error, trusted not in God Himself, but in the temple, as being the house of God. For almost after the manner of the Gentiles they worshipped Him in the temple. But learn how the Lord speaks, when abolishing it: "Who hath meted out heaven with a span, and the earth with his palm? Have not I?" "Thus says the Lord, Heaven is My throne, and the earth My footstool: what kind of house will ye build to Me, or what is the place of My rest?" Ye perceive that their hope is vain. Moreover, He again says, "Behold, they who have cast down this temple, even they shall build it up again." It has so happened. For through their going to war, it was destroyed by their enemies; and now: they, as the servants of their enemies, shall rebuild it. Again, it was revealed that the city and the temple and the people of Israel were to be given up. For the Scripture says, "And it shall come to pass in the last days, that the Lord will deliver up the sheep of His pasture, and their sheep-fold and tower, to destruction." And it so happened as the Lord had spoken. Let us inquire, then, if there still is a temple of God. There is—where He himself declared He would make and finish it. For it is written, "And it shall come to pass, when the week is completed, the temple of God shall be built in glory in the name of the Lord." I find, therefore, that a temple does exist. Learn, then, how it shall be built in the name of the Lord. Before we believed in God, the habitation of our heart was corrupt and weak, as being indeed like a temple made with hands. For it was full of idolatry, and was a habitation of demons, through our doing such things as were opposed to [the will of] God. But it shall be built, observe ye, in the name of the Lord, in order that the temple of the Lord may be built in glory. How? Learn [as follows]. Having received the forgiveness of sins, and placed our trust in the name of the Lord, we have become new creatures, formed again from the beginning. Wherefore in our habitation God truly dwells in us. How? His word of faith; His calling of promise; the wisdom of the statutes; the commands of the doctrine; He himself prophesying in us; He himself dwelling in us; opening to us who were enslaved by death the doors of the temple, that is, the mouth; and by giving us repentance introduced us into the incorruptible temple. He then, who wishes to be saved, looks not to man, but to Him who dwells in him, and speaks in him, amazed at never having either heard him utter such words with his mouth, nor himself having ever desired to hear them. This is the spiritual temple built for the Lord.

Chapter XVII.—Conclusion of the first part of the epistle.

As far as was possible, and could be done with perspicuity, I cherish the hope that, according to my desire, I have omitted none of those things at present [demanding consideration], which bear upon your salvation. For if I should write to you about things future, ye would not understand, because such knowledge is hid in parables. These things then are so.

Chapter XVIII.—Second part of the epistle.

The two ways. But let us now pass to another sort

of knowledge and doctrine. There are two ways of doctrine and authority, the one of light, and the other of darkness. But there is a great difference between these two ways. For over one are stationed the light-bringing angels of God, but over the other the angels of Satan. And He indeed (i.e., God) is Lord for ever and ever, but he (i.e., Satan) is prince of the time of iniquity.

Chapter XIX.—The way of light.

The way of light, then, is as follows. If anyone desires to travel to the appointed place, he must be zealous in his works. The knowledge, therefore, which is given to us for the purpose of walking in this way, is the following. Thou shalt love Him that created thee: thou shalt glorify Him that redeemed thee from death. Thou shalt be simple in heart, and rich in spirit. Thou shalt not join thyself to those who walk in the way of death. Thou shalt hate doing what is unpleasing to God: thou shalt hate all hypocrisy. Thou shalt not forsake the commandments of the Lord. Thou shalt not exalt thyself, but shalt be of a lowly mind. Thou shalt not take glory to thyself. Thou shalt not take evil counsel against thy neighbor. Thou shalt not allow over-boldness to enter into thy soul. Thou shalt not commit fornication: thou shalt not commit adultery: thou shalt not be a corrupter of youth. Thou shalt not let the word of God issue from thy lips with any kind of impurity. Thou shalt not accept persons when thou reproves any one for transgression. Thou shalt be meek: thou shalt be peaceable. Thou shalt tremble at the words which thou hears. Thou shalt not be mindful of evil against thy brother. Thou shalt not be of doubtful mind as to whether a thing shall be or not. Thou shalt not take the name of the Lord in vain. Thou shalt love thy neighbor more than thine own soul. Thou shalt not slay the child by procuring abortion; nor, again, shalt thou destroy it after it is born. Thou shalt not withdraw thy hand from thy son, or from thy daughter, but from their infancy thou shalt teach them the fear of the Lord. Thou shalt not covet what is thy neighbor's, nor shalt thou be avaricious. Thou shalt not be joined in soul with the haughty, but thou shalt be reckoned with the righteous and lowly. Receive thou as good things the trials which come upon thee. Thou shalt not be of double mind or of double tongue, for a double tongue is a snare of death. Thou shalt be subject to the Lord, and to [other] masters as the image of God, with modesty and fear. Thou shalt not issue orders with bitterness to thy maidservant or thy man-servant, who trust in the same [God], lest thou should not reverence that God who is above both; for He came to call men not according to their outward appearance, but according as the Spirit had prepared them. Thou shalt communicate in all things with thy neighbor; thou shalt not call things thine own; for if ye are partakers in common of things which are incorruptible, how much more [should you be] of those things which are corruptible! Thou shalt not be hasty with thy tongue, for the mouth is a snare of death. As far as possible, thou shalt be pure in thy soul. Do not be ready to stretch forth thy hands to take, whilst thou contracts them to give. Thou shalt love, as the apple of thine eye, everyone that speaks to thee the word of the Lord. Thou shalt remember the Day of Judgment, night and day. Thou shalt seek out every day the faces of the saints, either by word examining them, and going to exhort them, and meditating how to save a soul by the word, or by thy hands thou shalt labor for the redemption of thy sins. Thou shalt not hesitate to give, nor murmur when thou gives. "Give to everyone that asks thee," and thou shalt know who is the good Recompenser of the reward. Thou shalt preserve what thou hast received [in charge], neither adding to it nor taking from it. To the last thou shalt hate the wicked [one]. Thou shalt judge righteously. Thou shalt not make a schism, but thou shalt pacify those that contend by bringing them together. Thou shalt confess thy sins. Thou shalt not go to prayer with an evil conscience. This is the way of light.

Chapter XX.—The way of darkness.

But the way of darkness is crooked, and full of cursing; for it is the way of eternal death with punishment, in which way are the things that destroy the soul, viz., idolatry, over-confidence, the arrogance of power, hypocrisy, double-heartedness, adultery, murder, rapine, haughtiness, transgression, deceit, malice, self-sufficiency, poisoning, magic, avarice, want of the fear of God. [In this way, too,] are those who persecute the good, those who hate truth, those who love falsehood, those who know not the reward of righteousness, those who cleave not to that which is good, those who attend not with just judgment to the widow and orphan, those who watch not to the fear of God, [but incline] to wickedness, from whom meekness and patience are far off; persons who love vanity, follow after a reward, pity not the needy, labor not in aid of him who is overcome with toil; who are prone to evil-speaking, who know not Him that made them, who are murderers of children, destroyers of the workmanship of God; who turn away him that is in want, who oppress the afflicted, who are advocates of the rich, who are unjust judges of the poor, and who are in every respect transgressors.

Chapter XXI.—Conclusion.

It is well, therefore, that he who has learned the judgments of the Lord, as many as have been written, should walk in them. For he who keeps these shall be glorified in the kingdom of God; but he who chooses other things shall be destroyed with his works. On this account there will be a resurrection, on this account a retribution. I beseech you who are superiors, if you will receive any counsel of my good-will, have among yourselves those to whom you may show kindness: do not forsake them. For the day is at hand on which all things shall perish with the evil [one]. The Lord is near, and His reward. Again, and yet again, I beseech you: be good lawgivers to one another; continue faithful counsellors of one another; take away from among you all hypocrisy. And may God, who rules over all the world, give to you wisdom, intelligence, understanding, knowledge of His judgments, with patience. And be ye taught of God, inquiring diligently what the Lord asks from you; and do it that ye maybe safe in the Day of Judgment. And if you have any remembrance of what is good, be mindful of me, meditating on these things, in order that both my desire and watchfulness may result in some good. I beseech you, entreating this as a favor. While yet you are in this fair vessel, do not fail in any one of those things, but unceasingly seek after them, and fulfil every commandment; for these things are worthy. Wherefore I have been the more earnest to write to you, as my ability served, that I might cheer you. Farewell, ye children of love and peace. The Lord of glory and of all grace be with your spirit. Amen.

www.ingramcontent.com/pod-product-compliance
Lightning Source LLC
Chambersburg PA
CBHW052207070526
44585CB00017B/2107